How to Reprogram a Childs's Mind through the Power of Storytelling

The Loveday Method
Part 4

"The Magical Journey for Children"

The Fourth Book of a

Series of seven books.

A Heptalogy:
By
Geoffrey Loveday

How to Reprogram a Child's Mind

Author: Geoff Loveday

Text Copyright © Geoff Loveday (2022)

The right of Geoff Loveday to be identified as author of this work has been asserted by the author in accordance with section 77 and 78 of the Copyright, Designs and Patents Act 1988.

First Published in 2023

ISBN 978-1-83538-108-3 (Paperback)
     978-1-83538-109-0 (Hardback)
     978-1-83538-110-6 (E-Book)

Published by:
    Maple Publishers
    Fairbourne Drive, Atterbury,
    Milton Keynes,
    MK10 9RG, UK
    www.maplepublishers.com

> The book you're holding in your hands is a testament to the incredible power of a child's mind.
>
> The stories you are about to read are magical.
>
> The results may vary from person to person.

A CIP catalogue record for this title is available from the British Library.

All rights reserved. No part of this book may be reproduced or translated by any form or by any means, electronic or mechanical, including photocopying, recording or by any information storage and retrieval system without written permission from the author.

A must-read for children with unwanted thoughts that will give your child hope.

A journey into the stories of the mind.

I wonder where life will take us now...

And the journey begins.

Let me take you on this magical adventure.

Contents

Dedication 7

Acknowledgement & Inspiration 9

About the Author 10

A Journey into the Stories of the Mind 14

    The Power of Storytelling 14

    The Magic of Life 15

The Magical Childhood Voyage of Life 18

The Fairy of Imagination 22

Sarah and the Fairy of Hope 25

In the Realm of Nightmares 29

Bullying 33

    Jack's Story 34

    Leo's Inner Strength 36

    The Rabbit and the Oak 40

Anxiety and Fear 44

    The Power of Magic. 44

    The Land of Magic and Wonder 47

    Fear of the Dark 51

    Lea's Fear of Flying 55

Courage 60

    Courage and Facing Fear 60

    The Courage of a Child 63

Violence in the Home 67

Sadness 76

    The Magic Within 76

    The Magical Unicorn 77

Magical Journeys 80

    Jack's Magical Adventure 80

    A Magical Journey of a Lifetime 83

Obsessive-Compulsive Disorder (OCD) 87

Losing Someone We Love 91

    The Magical Mirror of Healing 91

    Childhood Trauma 94

Physical Pain 98

    Frequent and Debilitating Migraines 98

Shyness 101

Bravery 106

    A Dog Named Goldie. 106

    The Timid Mouse 108

    The Crystal Pendant 111

The Power of Knowledge 116

    The Treasure of the Mind… 116

    The Magical Talisman 121

    The Tree of Knowledge 124

    The Journey of Learning 127

The Meaning of Life. 132

Happiness: The Joy of Being Alive...136

The Storyteller's Tale..139

The Magical Forest 142

Becoming Calm 146

The Thirty-Day Challenge for Children....................................151

    How it Works..151

    Our Thoughts..153

    Mystical 30-Day Adventure 153

    Words of wisdom..157

Dedication

As I sat down to write this book, my thoughts drifted to the children of the world. Their laughter, their innocence, their boundless curiosity - these are the things that inspire me every day.

No matter where you go, you'll find children. In bustling cities and quiet villages, on sandy beaches and snowy mountain tops, in schools and playgrounds and homes. They are the future, the hope of our world.

And yet, so many children face unimaginable challenges. Poverty, war, disease, and discrimination - these are just a few of the obstacles that stand in their way. But even in the face of such adversity, they remain resilient, courageous, and full of hope.

So I want to dedicate this book to the beautiful children around the world. May it bring a smile to your face, a spark to your imagination, and a sense of wonder to your heart. May you know that you are loved, cherished, and valued - no matter who you are or where you come from.

And may we all work together to build a better world for our children, one that is safe, just, and full of opportunity. Because when we invest in our children, we invest in our future - and the future is bright, thanks to you.

Acknowledgement & Inspiration

I would like to express my gratitude to the people who made this book possible. First and foremost, I want to thank the brave children who have found a way to fight against the pain and suffering they are experiencing. Without their courage, this book would not have been possible.

I would like to express my gratitude to Capt. Martin C. Sanderson for his outstanding contribution to the book. His meticulous editing, proofreading, and finishing touches have made the book incredibly easy to read. Thank you for your dedication and hard work!

"This book is an inspiration to remarkable parents all over the world who selflessly devote themselves to nurturing and supporting their children's growth. Your unwavering dedication and guidance provide a safe haven for your children to thrive, and your love and understanding shape them into the incredible individuals they are meant to be. Your tireless efforts deserve recognition, and it is an honour to pay tribute to your invaluable contributions to the future of humanity."

About the Author

My name is Geoffrey Elliott Loveday

Inherited Therapy® and The Loveday Method® is one of my newest approaches to helping people overcome many of the problems and symptoms that are holding them back from living a happy and fulfilling life.

The Loveday Method is an advanced technique for travelling back in time through one's own consciousness in order to access dormant memories that are stored within one's DNA and are to blame for generational trauma.

The purpose of this treatment is to provide therapy for traumas that have been present in the family for a great many years and to uncover the mysteries that are hidden within our Genes and consciousness.

I am a full-time professional hypnotherapist and practitioner in pure–hypnoanalysis, as well as a Certified Hypnosis Instructor. And now, much to my surprise, I find myself the author of 4 books.

My previous three works explore the psyche and the effects of Transgenerational Trauma.

Now I've decided to write a children's book. This is writing designed to help a young mind develop its potential.

The book you're holding in your hands is a testament to the incredible power of a child's mind.

As someone who has delved deeply into the topics of the mind and transgenerational trauma, I'm thrilled to be taking a new approach with my latest project.

This children's book is all about harnessing the incredible power of imagination and creativity that every child possesses.

A must-read for children with unwanted thoughts which will give your child hope.

Are your child's unwanted thoughts causing them distress and anxiety? Our collection of must-read stories is here to help! These tales have been carefully crafted to inspire children and give them the courage to face their fears head-on.

By reading these stories to your child each night before bed, you'll be planting the seeds of hope and resilience in their subconscious mind. And as they sleep, their mind will continue to work on these ideas, helping to free them from the fears that have been holding them back.

So why wait? Dive into our captivating stories today and give your child the gift of confidence and peace of mind...

The Adventure of Life

Life is a wondrous journey, full of untold mysteries and enchanted moments. At every turn, there are new and magical opportunities waiting to be discovered - adventures that are just waiting to unfold.

Each day is a canvas, a blank slate upon which we can paint our hopes and dreams, using the brushes of our imagination and the colours of our hearts. We are the authors of our own stories, the magicians of our own destiny, weaving a tapestry of magic that is uniquely our own.

And as we venture forth into the unknown, we are filled with a sense of wonder and awe, for we know that there are secrets waiting to be uncovered, treasures waiting to be discovered. We are eager to explore the world around us, to embrace the unknown and to discover the limitless possibilities that life has to offer.

So let us embark on this great adventure, with hearts full of hope and minds open to the mysteries of the universe. For in this journey of life, there is magic waiting to be found, wonder waiting to be experienced, and joy waiting to be shared. Let us embrace the adventure of life, and see where it takes us.

A Journey into the Stories of the Mind

The Power of Storytelling

As you embark on the journey of this book, I can't help but wonder about the emotions that are swirling within you. How are you truly feeling at this moment?

Perhaps as you delve deeper into these pages, you'll uncover a story that resonates with your soul and sheds light on the shadows of unhappiness that you may be harbouring.

Allow yourself to be swept away by the power of storytelling and the transformative magic that lies within.

The Magic of Life

Life itself is a wonderful and magical thing. Every living being, no matter how small or large, is a remarkable product of nature and the universe. Life is full of mysteries, complexities, and beauty. From the tiniest microorganisms to the towering trees and majestic animals, each one has its unique characteristics and plays a crucial role in the ecosystem.

The magic of life is not just about physical existence, but also about the experiences and emotions that come along with it. Love, joy, friendship, and other feelings are all part of the magic of life. Each moment is unique and fleeting, and we have the power to make the most of them by cherishing the people and experiences that matter most to us.

Life is full of wonders, and there is so much to explore and discover. From the depths of the oceans to the highest mountains, there are endless opportunities to experience and appreciate the magic of life. It's up to us to seek out those experiences and embrace the wonder that surrounds us.

The stories you are about to read are magical. They will allow your child the hope that they need to overcome any issue that is affecting them by using the power of the mind and their imagination.

"Using your imagination as your compass and your mind as your guide, you'll discover that anything is possible.
Geoffrey E Loveday

Step into the world of enchantment and let your mind wander through these captivating tales. With each turn of the page, you will find yourself transported to a realm where magic exists and anything is possible. These stories have the power to ignite your imagination, to inspire your mind, and to unlock the hidden potential within you.

As you journey through these pages, you will discover that no challenge is too great, and no obstacle too daunting. For within the pages of this book, you will find the tools you need to overcome any issue that life may throw your way. So come, let us delve into this mystical world together, and let us see what wonders await us.

Young readers; this book is a treasure map to help you navigate through life's challenges. With your imagination as your compass and your mind as your guide, you'll discover that anything is possible. So take a deep breath, open your heart, and embark on this exciting journey with me.

The Magical Childhood Voyage of Life

Once upon a time, in a far-off land, there was a magical voyage of life that all children must take. It was a journey that every child went on, and it was full of wonder, adventure, and discovery.

At the beginning of the journey, each child was given a magical map.

This map was unique to them, and it showed them the path they must take to discover their true selves. The map was full of twists and turns, and it was up to the child to decide which path to take.

As they set out on their journey, the children encountered all sorts of challenges and obstacles. Some were big and scary, like the dark forests that seemed to stretch on forever. Others were smaller, like the rivers they had to cross or the mountains they had to climb.

But the children were not alone on their journey. They had companions to help them along the way. There were talking animals, like wise old owls and friendly squirrels, who would offer them advice and guidance. And there were other children, too, who were also on their own magical voyages. Together, they shared stories and songs, and they helped each other overcome their fears.

As the children continued on their journey, they discovered all sorts of wondrous things. They found hidden caves filled with treasure, sparkling waterfalls that sparkled in the sunlight, and meadows filled with wildflowers that swayed in the breeze.

But perhaps the greatest discovery the children made was the discovery of themselves. Along the way, they learned about their own strengths and weaknesses, their own likes and dislikes. They learned what made them happy, and what made them sad. And they learned that, no matter what happened, they could always find their way back home.

Eventually, the children's magical voyage of life came to an end. They had reached the end of their journey, and they had discovered all there was to discover. But even though the journey was over, the memories and lessons they had learned would stay with them forever.

And so, as they returned home, the children knew that they had grown and changed, and that they were ready for whatever adventures life had in store for them next. They knew that they would always be guided by the lessons they had learned on their magical voyage of life.

The Fairy of Imagination

Let me take you to the magical kingdom to show you the power of your imagination.

In a magical kingdom far away, lived a young girl named Susanna. Susanna was brave, kind, and curious, but she often felt lost and uncertain about the world around her. One day, while exploring the kingdom, she discovered a hidden library filled with mysterious books.

As she browsed through the books, she came across a shimmering tome that seemed to glow with its own light. As she opened it, a beautiful fairy appeared before her.

"Greetings, young Susanna," said the fairy. "I am the fairy of imagination, and I have been waiting for someone like you. This book contains a special kind of magic - the power of imagination. With it, you can overcome any fears or doubts and achieve anything you set your mind to."

Overjoyed, Susanna eagerly read the book from cover to cover. The fairy showed her how to use the magic within her mind to create a world full of wonder and possibility. They journeyed together through the pages of the book, encountering dragons, unicorns, and other magical creatures.

As they travelled, Susanna's confidence grew, and she learned to trust herself and believe in her abilities. She became braver and more adventurous than ever before, and her mind opened up to endless possibilities.

When the adventure was over and Susanna closed the book, she looked out into the kingdom and saw it with fresh eyes. She realised that the power of imagination was within her all along and that anything was possible if she just believed in herself.

From that day forward, Susanna lived her life with a sense of magic and wonder, always eager to explore and discover new horizons. And she knew that no matter what challenges lay ahead, she had the power of her imagination to guide her through.

Sarah and the Fairy of Hope

Are you looking for a magical story that can inspire children to use their imagination and overcome any obstacle?

Here's a story that might help...

In a far-off land, there lived a young girl named Sarah. Sarah was a dreamer, and she spent most of her time lost in her imagination, imagining all sorts of magical adventures. But one day, something happened that made her lose hope and joy.

Sarah's father had lost his job, and the family was struggling to make ends meet. They had to move to a small apartment, and Sarah had to change schools. She was feeling sad and lonely and didn't know how to cope with the changes in her life.

One night, as she was lying in bed, unable to sleep, she noticed a small light flickering in the corner of her room. Curious, she got up and followed the light. It led her to a tiny door that she had never noticed before. Sarah opened the door, and to her amazement, she found herself in a magical forest.

The trees were made of candy, and the leaves were made of chocolate. The flowers were giant lollipops, and the air was filled with the sweetest scent she had ever smelled. She could hear the sound of a river, and she followed the sound until she found a crystal-clear stream. She put her hand in the water, and to her surprise, she felt a surge of energy flowing through her body.

As she walked along the stream, she saw a small figure coming towards her. It was a fairy, and she introduced herself as Hope. Hope asked Sarah what was troubling her, and Sarah poured out her heart to the fairy. Hope listened patiently and then said, "Sarah, I can see that you are a dreamer, and you have a powerful imagination. You have the power to create your reality. All you need is to believe in yourself and your dreams."

Sarah didn't understand what Hope meant, but the fairy smiled and said, "Close your eyes and imagine the life you want to live. Imagine the things you want to do, the places you want to see, and the people you want to meet. Imagine that you already have everything you need to make your dreams come true. Can you see it?"

Sarah closed her eyes and let her imagination take over. She saw herself living in a big house, with her family, surrounded by all her favourite things. She saw herself travelling the world, meeting new people, and having amazing adventures. She felt happy, confident, and full of hope.

When she opened her eyes, she was back in her room. The light was still flickering, but now she understood its meaning. The light represented hope, and it was always within her reach. She closed her eyes again and imagined her dream life. She felt the same surge of energy she had felt in the magical forest, and she knew that anything was possible.

From that day on, Sarah never lost her hope and joy again. She knew that she had the power to create her reality, and she used her imagination to overcome any obstacle that came her way. She lived a magical life, full of adventures, love, and happiness, and she never forgot the lesson she had learned from Hope, the fairy of hope.

In the Realm of Nightmares

Let's explore the unsettling realm of nightmares and their profound impact on our children. You can discover effective strategies to transform their mind-set and overcome these night terrors by harnessing the power of their imagination.

Once upon a time, in a land of enchantment, there was a young girl named Emilia who suffered from terrible nightmares every night. She would wake up in a cold sweat, trembling with fear, and unable to fall back asleep.

Emilia's parents were at a loss as to how to help their daughter, and so they decided to seek the advice of a wise old owl who lived deep in the heart of the forest.

The owl listened patiently as Emilia's parents told him about their daughter's nightmares. Then he nodded thoughtfully and said, "I know just what to do."

The owl led Emilia's parents to a small clearing in the forest, where he instructed them to build a bonfire and surround it with special stones that would harness the power of the fire.

As the fire burned brightly, the owl began to chant and incantation that called upon the spirits of the forest to aid them in their quest. Emilia watched in amazement as the flames grew higher and the stones began to glow with a radiant light.

Then, the owl turned to Emilia and said, "These stones will protect you from your nightmares. Carry them with you always, and you will sleep soundly and peacefully every night."

Emilia thanked the owl and her parents and promised to never forget the magic of the forest. She held the stones close to her heart and knew that they would keep her safe from the terrors of the night.

From that day forward, Emilia slept soundly every night, free from the nightmares that had once haunted her. She knew that the magic of the forest had saved her from her fears, and she was forever grateful to the wise old owl for his guidance and wisdom.

And so, Emilia grew up to be a strong and courageous woman, always carrying the stones with her as a reminder of the magic that lay within her heart. She used the lessons she had learned from the owl and the forest to help others overcome their fears and find the courage to face their own challenges. had been imbued with ancient magic.

Bullying

Uncover the insidious effects of bullying on our children well into adulthood. Empower them to rise above the scars of their past by unlocking the boundless potential of their minds and imagination.

One way we can help our children combat bullying is through the power of the mind and imagination. By encouraging our children to develop a positive self-image, and to visualise themselves as strong, capable, and confident, we can help them build the inner resilience and strength they need to face life's challenges head-on.

Through guided meditation, visualisation exercises, and positive affirmations, we can help our children to tap into the power of their own minds and create a reality in which they are safe, happy, and free from harm. We can encourage them to visualise themselves standing up to bullies, speaking up for themselves and others, and walking away from harmful situations with their heads held high.

In doing so, we can empower our children to take control of their own lives and to create a reality in which bullying no longer has a hold on them. We can teach them that they are the masters of their own destinies and that no matter what life throws their way, they have the strength and courage to overcome it.

Jack's Story

In a small town nestled amidst rolling hills and sparkling streams, there was a young boy named Jack.

Jack was a gentle soul, with a heart as big as the sky and a smile that could light up even the darkest of days. Yet despite his kind nature, Jack found himself the target of bullies at his school. Every day, he would dread going to class, knowing that he would be met with jeers and taunts from his tormentors.

One day, as Jack was wandering through the woods near his home, he stumbled upon an old tree unlike any he had ever seen before. Its bark was gnarled and twisted, and its branches reached up to the sky like a hundred crooked fingers. As he approached the tree, he felt a strange energy pulsing through the air around him, like a gentle breeze that whispered secrets in his ear.

With a sense of curiosity and wonder, Jack reached out and touched the tree's rough bark. Suddenly, a burst of light enveloped him, and he found himself transported to a magical realm, where fairies flitted through the air and unicorns roamed free.

In this enchanted world, Jack felt a sense of peace and tranquillity wash over him. The worries and fears that had plagued him for so long melted away, and he was filled with a sense of joy and wondered that he had never experienced before.

As he explored this magical realm, Jack discovered a small stream that flowed through the heart of the forest. As he dipped his toes into the cool, clear water, he felt a sense of inner peace wash over him, like a warm blanket on a chilly night.

From that day forward, whenever he felt afraid or alone, Jack would return to the magical forest and immerse himself in its peaceful embrace. With the help of the fairies and unicorns, he learned to overcome his fears and find the strength within himself to face life's challenges with courage and grace.

And though he still encountered bullies from time to time, he no longer felt powerless in their presence, for he knew that deep within himself lay a magical world of wonder and beauty, a world where anything was possible and where he could find the inner peace and strength to overcome any obstacle that came his way.

Leo's Inner Strength

In a small village nestled in a valley surrounded by mountains, there was a child named Leo.

Leo was a kind-hearted and imaginative boy who loved to explore the world around him. He was always curious and eager to learn new things.

However, Leo had a problem. He was being bullied by a group of older children who would make fun of him and tease him relentlessly. They would call him names and push him around, and it made Leo feel scared and powerless.

One day, Leo decided that he had had enough. He went into the forest that bordered the village, hoping to find a way to overcome his fear and stand up to his bullies.

As he wandered deeper into the woods, he came across a clearing that he had never seen before. In the centre of the clearing stood a magnificent tree, its branches reaching up to the sky.

As Leo approached the tree, he heard a soft voice whispering his name. He looked around, but he couldn't see anyone. The voice spoke again, urging him to come closer to the tree. Leo felt a little nervous, but he also felt drawn to the tree. He stepped forward, and as he did, he felt a strange energy envelop him.

Suddenly, Leo was transported to a magical world. The tree had taken him to a realm where anything was possible. He saw a rainbow-coloured river, a castle made of candy, and a forest full of talking animals.

Leo was amazed, and he felt a sense of wonder and joy that he had never experienced before. As he explored this magical world, Leo encountered a wise old wizard who offered to help him overcome his fear.

The wizard gave Leo a magic wand and taught him how to use it to defend himself.

He showed him how to summon a shield to protect himself from harm and how to cast a spell to make his bullies fall asleep.

Armed with his new magical powers, Leo returned to the village. He faced his bullies with confidence and courage, knowing that he had the ability to defend himself. The older children were surprised by his newfound strength, and they soon learned to respect him instead of teasing him.

From that day on, Leo was no longer afraid. He had found a way to overcome his fear and stand up to his bullies. And whenever he needed a little extra courage, he would simply close his eyes and remember the magic of the tree and the wizard who had helped him.

The Rabbit and the Oak

The courage of a little Rabbit called Milo...

In a magical forest, there lived a timid little rabbit named Milo.

Milo was constantly picked on by a gang of mischievous fairies who loved to play pranks on him and make him feel small and insignificant.

One day, while wandering through the forest, Milo stumbled upon a wise old fairy who saw the sadness in his eyes and took pity on him. The fairy gave Milo a magical acorn and told him that if he planted it in the ground and watered it with his tears, it would grow into a tree that would give him the courage he needed to stand up to the bullies.

Milo did as he was told, and soon the acorn sprouted into a mighty oak tree, tall and strong. Milo climbed up into the tree and drank from a magical stream that flowed from its roots, filling him with a newfound sense of bravery.

With his newfound courage, Milo confronted the mischievous fairies who had been picking on him. They laughed and teased him at first, but then Milo summoned his courage and stood up to them, telling them that he would no longer allow them to bully him.

The fairies were surprised by Milo's newfound bravery, and they were ashamed of the way they had treated him. From that day on, they treated Milo with kindness and respect, and he became a hero in the eyes of all the creatures of the forest.

And so, dear friends, let this tale remind you that even the smallest and meekest among us can find the courage they need to stand up for themselves, thanks to the magic that lives within us all.

Anxiety and Fear

Anxiety has the formidable ability to terrify and overwhelm our children.

The Power of Magic.

Once upon a time, there lived a little girl named Lea. She was a bright and curious child, always eager to explore the world around her. But one day, something strange happened.

Lea woke up one morning feeling afraid. She had never felt this way before, and she didn't know why. Her parents tried to comfort her, but she couldn't shake the feeling of anxiety that had settled in her chest.

They took her to see the doctors, but none of them knew how to deal with this problem because Lea was so young. They tried everything they could think of, but nothing seemed to work.

Lea was afraid to go to sleep at night, and even during the day, she felt like something was always lurking in the shadows. But she had something that the doctors didn't know about - an amazing imagination.

As she lay in bed one night, trying to calm her racing thoughts, Lea closed her eyes and began to imagine a magical world. In this world, she was the hero of her own story, and nothing could harm her.

She imagined a land of wonder and enchantment, filled with talking animals and friendly wizards. The sky was a brilliant shade of pink, and the trees glowed with a warm, golden light.

As she explored this new world, Lea felt her anxiety melting away.

With each passing day, Lea's imagination grew stronger. She began to imagine new and exciting adventures, each one more daring than the last. She fought dragons, saved princesses, and explored hidden caves filled with treasure.

Through the power of her imagination, Lea learned to face her fears and overcome her anxiety. She no longer woke up in the middle of the night, afraid of the shadows. Instead, she looked forward to her next adventure in her magical world.

And as she grew older, Lea never forgot the lessons she learned from her imagination. She knew that no matter what challenges life threw her way, she had the power to overcome them with the strength of her own mind. And that, my friends, is the power of magic.

The Land of Magic and Wonder

There was a young girl named Anna who lived in a world full of magic and wonder.

She loved nothing more than exploring the enchanted forests and playing with the talking animals that lived there.

But as she grew older, Anna began to feel a growing sense of anxiety and fear. She found herself constantly checking and rechecking things, worried that she had forgotten something important. She tried to ignore these feelings, but they only grew stronger.

One day, as she was wandering through the woods, Anna came across a wise old owl who sensed her distress and offered to help her.

The owl told her that the key to overcoming her fears was to learn to trust in her own inner strength and wisdom.

Anna didn't know what that meant, but the owl promised to guide her on a journey of self-discovery that would help her find the answers she sought. So, with a mixture of excitement and trepidation, Anna set out on her quest.

As she journeyed through the woods, Anna encountered many challenges and obstacles. At one point, she found herself in a dark and foreboding cave, where her OCD was triggered by the darkness and the echoing sounds. She wanted to turn back, but the owl urged her on.

Slowly but surely, Anna began to learn new things about herself. She discovered that she was braver and stronger than she ever thought possible. She learned to trust in her instincts and intuition and to believe in herself even when things seemed impossible.

Finally, after many months of travel, Anna reached a clearing in the woods where the sun shone bright and warm. There, she found the wise old owl waiting for her, surrounded by a circle of glowing crystals.

The owl told her that the crystals represented her own inner strength and wisdom and that she had the power to draw on them whenever she needed to. Anna didn't understand how this could help her overcome her OCD, but the owl urged her to try.

So Anna closed her eyes, and with a deep breath, she reached out to touch one of the glowing crystals. As she did, she felt a surge of energy flow through her body, washing away her fears and doubts.

From that moment on, Anna knew that she had the power within her to overcome any obstacle that came her way. She had discovered the magic of self-belief, and nothing would ever hold her back again.

Fear of the Dark

We look at our children and think they have no worries or fears, but what if one day they came to us and said they were afraid of the dark? As parents, we would want to do everything in our power to make sure our children felt safe and secure. We never think they have the same worries as an adult, but what if they do?

As a magical storyteller, I would like to share a tale that may help answer your question.

Once upon a time, in a land far, far away, there lived a little boy named Max. He was a bright young child, always eager to explore the world around him. But one day, something changed. Max began to fear the dark.

At first, his parents thought it was just a passing phase. But as the days turned into weeks, they realised it was something more. Max refused to go to bed without a nightlight, and even then, he would wake up in the middle of the night, crying out for his parents.

His parents tried everything they could think of to help him. They tried to reason with him, to show him that there was nothing to be afraid of. They even tried scolding him, telling him that he was being silly. But nothing seemed to work.

Finally, one day, Max's grandfather came to visit. He was a wise man, with a heart full of love and a mind full of magic. He sat down with Max and asked him what he was afraid of.

"I don't know," Max replied. "I just feel like something is watching me in the dark."

His grandfather smiled, then took his hand and led him outside. They sat on the grass, under a starry sky.

"Look up at the stars, Max," his grandfather said. "Each one is a light in the darkness. And just like those stars, there is a light inside of you that can shine, even when things seem dark."

He explained to Max that fear was a natural part of life, but that it didn't have to control him. He showed him that there was always a way to find light in the darkness, whether it was through the warmth of a loved one's embrace, the comfort of a favourite toy, or the power of his own imagination.

From that day on, Max began to see the world in a new light. He still felt afraid of the dark sometimes, but now he knew that he had the power to overcome that fear. And when he felt lost or alone, he would look up at the stars and remember the light that shone inside of him.

As parents, it's important to remember that our children have worries and fears, just like we do. But with a little love and a touch of magic, we can help them find their way through the darkness and into the light.

These two stories were taken from my third book, and are very relevant here.

We can find a way, by using the power of their imagination, to take them on a magical journey to free them from the suffering they are going through.

Lea's Fear of Flying

Lea was a curious and adventurous child, but she had one fear that held her back: she was afraid of flying. Every time her family went on a trip that required flying, Lea would become anxious and scared, and her parents could see the fear in her eyes.

One day, while Lea was exploring the woods near her home, she stumbled upon a strange, glowing tree. As she approached it, she felt warmth spreading through her body and suddenly, she found herself in a magical world.

Lea looked around in amazement as she saw colourful creatures she had never seen before. She walked through the lush, green forest and eventually came across a kind and wise fairy who asked what had brought her to this enchanted land.

Lea opened up to the fairy and told her about her fear of flying. The fairy listened intently and then gave her a magical feather. "This feather," the fairy said, "will help you conquer your fear of flying. Whenever you feel scared or anxious, hold onto this feather, and it will take you wherever you want to go."

With the feather in her hand, Lea felt brave and empowered. She closed her eyes, held onto the feather, and felt herself lifting off the ground. As she opened her eyes, she saw the world from a completely different perspective. She saw the vastness of the land, the endless blue of the sky, and the beauty of nature below.

Lea felt a sense of wonder and exhilaration as she soared through the clouds. She felt free and alive, and her fear of flying disappeared. She landed safely back in the magical world, where the fairy was waiting for her.

"Did the feather help you?" the fairy asked.

"Yes," Lea said with a smile. "I am not afraid anymore."

The fairy smiled back and said, "Remember, Lea, courage is not the absence of fear, but the willingness to face it. You have shown great bravery today."

Lea returned home with newfound confidence and a deep appreciation for the magic of the world. She knew that she could conquer any fear as long as she had the courage to face it. And whenever she felt scared, she would hold onto the magical feather and remember the wonderful adventure that had set her free.

Courage

Courage is not the absence of fear, but the willingness to face what lies ahead despite the fear you are feeling.

Courage and Facing Fear

In a land of wizards and witches, there was a young sorcerer named Alex. Despite his magical abilities, Alex had always been afraid of the dark. He would jump at the slightest sound and imagine all sorts of terrifying creatures lurking in the shadows.

One day, his father, a wise old wizard, called him to his study. "My dear son," he said, "I know you're afraid of the dark, but fear is not something to be ashamed of. In fact, it's an opportunity to be courageous."

Alex was confused. "But how can fear make me courageous?" he asked.

His father smiled. "Courage is not the absence of fear, my son. It's the willingness to face it. And that's what I want you to do. I want you to confront your fear and find the magic within it."

With his father's words ringing in his ears, Alex set out on a quest to conquer his fear. He travelled deep into the forest, where the darkness was thickest, and there he found a mysterious cave.

Without hesitation, he entered the cave, his wand at the ready. As he walked deeper and deeper, the darkness seemed to grow thicker and more menacing. Alex felt his heart pounding in his chest, and his hands were shaking.

But he didn't stop. He kept walking, step by step until he finally reached the heart of the cave. And there, in the middle of the darkness, he found a glowing crystal.

The crystal was surrounded by a powerful aura, and Alex knew that he had to be careful. But he also knew that he had to be brave. He approached the crystal, and as he got closer, he felt a warm glow envelop him.

And then something amazing happened. Alex felt his fear melting away, replaced by a newfound sense of courage and strength. He realised that his fear had been holding him back, but now he was free.

With his newfound courage, Alex returned to his village a hero. He no longer feared the dark, and he was ready to face any challenge that came his way.

And so he lived happily ever after, knowing that true courage comes not from being fearless, but from facing one's fears head-on.

The Courage of a Child

In a far-off kingdom, there lived a young boy named Jack. Jack was a kind-hearted child with a fierce spirit that always seemed to shine through. He was an orphan, but he didn't let that define him. Instead, he used his difficult past as a source of inner strength and courage.

One day, an evil sorcerer descended upon the kingdom, casting a spell that enveloped everything in darkness. The sorcerer declared that he would only lift the spell if the kingdom gave him their most precious treasure - the golden flower that bloomed in the palace garden. The flower was said to hold magical properties that the sorcerer coveted.

The king was in a state of panic and ordered his soldiers to retrieve the flower. But Jack, who had overheard the conversation, knew that the flower held a deeper meaning to the kingdom's people. It was the symbol of hope and happiness, and without it, the people would lose all hope.

Determined to save the flower and the kingdom, Jack set out on a perilous journey to the sorcerer's lair. Armed with only his courage and inner strength, he faced many challenges on his way. He had to cross treacherous rivers, climb steep mountains, and battle fierce creatures that stood in his way.

But Jack never lost heart. He believed in his cause and drew upon his inner strength to overcome each obstacle. As he reached the sorcerer's lair, he found himself face-to-face with the evil sorcerer.

The sorcerer tried to intimidate Jack, but Jack stood his ground. With a steely determination, he refused to give in to the sorcerer's demands. The sorcerer grew angry and raised his wand to cast a spell, but Jack was ready. He pulled out a small vial of liquid and threw it at the sorcerer, causing the wand to shatter.

With the sorcerer defeated, the kingdom was bathed in a warm glow, and the golden flower bloomed once more. The people cheered, and the king declared Jack a hero for his bravery and determination. From that day on, Jack was known throughout the land as the child with the inner strength to fight back against the darkness.

And so, the kingdom thrived, and Jack continued to inspire others with his courage and unwavering spirit. His story was told for generations, reminding everyone that no matter how dark things may seem, there is always hope and inner strength to fight back.

Violence in the Home

...and the effect it has on our children

In a far-off land, there was a young girl named Sofia. She lived in a beautiful house with her parents, but their home was filled with anger and violence.

Every day, Sofia heard her parents fighting and shouting at each other. She would often hide under her bed, trembling with fear, waiting for the storm to pass.

One day, as she lay under her bed, she closed her eyes and began to imagine a world without violence. She pictured herself in a magical forest, surrounded by colourful trees and sparkling streams. Suddenly, a magical fairy appeared before her.

The fairy saw Sofia's sadness and asked her what was wrong. Sofia shared her story and told the fairy about the violence in her home. The fairy listened intently and then gave Sofia a magical wand. "With this wand, you can create a world without violence," she said.

Sofia hesitated at first, not sure if she could really do it. But then, she closed her eyes, held the wand tightly, and imagined a world without violence.

She waved the wand, and suddenly, the world around her transformed. The trees glowed with vibrant colours, and the streams sparkled like diamonds.

Excited by her newfound power, Sofia began to explore her magical world. She met friendly creatures and made new friends. She even found a wise old owl who taught her the importance of forgiveness and compassion.

As Sofia continued to explore her magical world, she felt her heart begin to heal. She no longer felt the pain and fear that had consumed her for so long.

She knew that she could never change the world outside her magical forest, but she also knew that she could always return to her magical world whenever she needed to feel safe and loved.

Years passed, and Sofia grew up to be a kind and compassionate woman. She used the lessons she learned in her magical world to help others who were suffering from violence and abuse. She knew that the power of imagination was a magical gift that could help heal the wounds of the soul and bring hope to those who felt lost and alone.

And so, the legend of Sofia's magical world lived on, inspiring others to find their own magic within and to use their imagination to create a world without violence.

The Celestial Connection

A Magical Voyage to Heal the Heart

In the mystical land of Luminara, a place where the stars shone brighter than anywhere else, there was a secret art known as Stellar Soul Healing.

This ancient practice allowed one to journey beyond the physical realm, unlocking the mysteries of the mind to mend the wounds left by loss and grief.

Aria, a young healer in Luminara, had a unique gift. She could hear the whispers of the stars, their celestial melodies guiding her path.

When her beloved sister, Lyra, passed away, Aria's heart shattered into a thousand pieces, leaving her with a feeling of deep, unrelenting sorrow. In her darkest moments, she longed to find solace and to heal her broken heart.

One starry night, as Aria gazed at the heavens, a brilliant shooting star streaked across the sky, leaving a trail of sparkling stardust.

Entranced, she followed the shimmering trail to a hidden grove, where she discovered an ancient, celestial tome.

This was the Book of Stellar Soul Healing, a sacred text containing the wisdom of the stars that her ancestors had first written down the secret art they had practiced for centuries.

As Aria immersed herself in the book's teachings, she discovered that the connection between the living and the departed was not severed, but instead transcended time and space. The key to healing her heartache lay within the mysteries of the mind and the power of the stars.

With newfound determination, Aria embarked on a magical voyage to the Celestial Realm, guided by the melodies of the stars. As she journeyed through the cosmos, she encountered wondrous beings and celestial landscapes, each reflecting her inner emotions and the memories she held dear.

In the heart of the Celestial Realm, Aria found the Garden of Remembrance, a radiant haven where the souls of the departed could reunite with their loved ones. There, among the blossoms of ethereal starflowers, she found Lyra, her sister's luminous spirit waiting to embrace her.

As Aria and Lyra reunited, their love transcended the boundaries of the physical world, soothing the pain that had engulfed Aria's heart. The sisters shared stories and laughter, their celestial connection mending the wounds left by loss and grief.

As their time in the Garden of Remembrance drew to a close, Lyra bestowed upon Aria a sacred gift: a gleaming star crystal that held the essence of their bond. With this treasure, Aria would always carry a piece of her sister's love and the knowledge that their connection was eternal.

Aria returned to Luminara, her heart lighter and filled with newfound hope. She dedicated her life to sharing the magic of Stellar Soul Healing, guiding others on their celestial voyages to heal the heartache left by the loss of their loved ones.

As a result, Luminara's star knowledge kept shining, serving as a reminder of the strength of love and the indestructible ties that bind us all across space and time.

The fictional works I've given are meant to arouse a feeling of awe and enchantment. Although the story is fiction, it does touch on topics that have real-world applications, including the significance of self-discovery and the strength of the mind. The story's central ideas can motivate us to investigate the possibilities of our own minds and the effects that our thoughts and feelings can have on our well-being, even though the magical elements are fictional.

Sadness

These stories tell of the sadness of two children and how, by using magic and reversing their thoughts, they found true happiness.

The Magic Within

One misty morning, a little girl woke up feeling a heavy weight upon her heart. She couldn't quite put her finger on what was wrong, but a deep sadness consumed her. As she gazed out her window, she saw a flash of light and heard a whisper on the wind. It was a magical fairy, beckoning her to come outside.

With trepidation, the little girl stepped outside and was greeted by a wondrous sight. The forest was alive with glittering fireflies, and the trees were swaying to the rhythm of an invisible orchestra. The fairy fluttered around her, sprinkling stardust on her hair and whispering words of comfort.

As the little girl closed her eyes and breathed in the enchanted air, she felt a stirring within her mind. She remembered the power of her thoughts, and how she could use them to transform her reality. With a deep breath, she focused on positive thoughts and imagined herself surrounded by love, joy, and peace.

The fairy smiled, knowing that the little girl had rediscovered the magic within her. And as the sun broke through the mist, the little girl felt the sadness lift and saw the world in a new light. From that day on, she knew that the power of her mind could overcome any obstacle and bring her joy and wonder beyond measure.

The Magical Unicorn

There was a little girl named Janie who had been feeling sad for a long time. She didn't know why she felt this way, but everything seemed gloomy and she didn't have much interest in playing with her toys or spending time with her friends.

One day, as she was wandering through the forest near her house, she stumbled upon a magical unicorn. It was a beautiful creature, with a sparkling coat and a gentle demeanour. The unicorn noticed that Janie looked sad and asked her what was wrong.

Janie told the unicorn about her feelings of sadness and how she couldn't shake them off no matter how hard she tried. The unicorn listened carefully and then said, "I have a magic spell that can help you turn your thoughts around. Would you like me to try it on you?"

Janie nodded eagerly, and the unicorn closed its eyes and focused its energy. Suddenly, Janie's thoughts began to change. Instead of dwelling on negative things, she began to think about all the good things in her life, like her family, her friends, and her pets. She remembered all the fun times she had playing with her toys and going on adventures with her friends.

As she thought about these things, her mood began to lift, and she felt lighter and happier than she had in a long time. She thanked the unicorn for its help and skipped happily back home, eager to share her newfound happiness with her loved ones.

From that day on, Janie made a habit of focusing on the positive things in her life, and whenever she felt sad or down, she would remember the magical spell that the unicorn had taught her and find happiness once again. And she lived happily ever after.

Magical Journeys

Jack's Magical Adventure

There was a little boy named Jack. Jack was a curious and adventurous child who loved to explore the world around him. One day, as he was playing in the woods near his house, he stumbled upon a mysterious object hidden under a bush.

As he pulled the object out, he realised it was a magical key with a note attached to it. The note read, "This key will unlock the door to a magical adventure. Follow the clues and discover the wonders that await you."

Excited by the possibilities, Jack set out on his adventure, following the clues and exploring the world around him. He journeyed through dark forests, across vast oceans, and up towering mountains. Along the way, he met a host of magical creatures, from fairies and unicorns to dragons and giants.

Despite the challenges he faced, Jack never lost his sense of wonder and curiosity. He continued on his journey, determined to uncover the secrets that lay ahead.

Finally, after many long days and nights of travelling, Jack arrived at the end of his adventure. He found himself standing in front of a massive door, adorned with intricate carvings and sparkling jewels. Using the magical key he had found, Jack unlocked the door and stepped inside.

What he found inside was beyond his wildest dreams. A vast hall filled with wonders, from glittering treasures to magical artefacts and ancient books. Jack spent hours exploring, marvelling at the incredible sights and sounds that surrounded him.

At last, as the sun began to set, Jack knew it was time to go home. As he walked out of the hall, he felt a sense of satisfaction and fulfilment he had never known before. He knew that, no matter where his adventures took him next, he would always carry the magic of this incredible journey with him.

A Magical Journey of a Lifetime

Once upon a time, in a world far away, there was a young child who was about to embark on a magical journey of a lifetime. This child, whose name was Rachel, had always dreamed of adventure and excitement, and little did she know, her wish was about to come true.

As she stepped out of her cosy home and into the bright sunlight of a new day, she felt a sense of anticipation that she had never experienced before. The birds sang sweetly in the trees, and the flowers bloomed in a rainbow of colours as if welcoming her on her journey.

Rachel set out on her journey, and as she walked, she encountered many magical creatures. There were talking animals that could walk and talk like humans, fairies that fluttered around her head, and even a friendly dragon that soared high in the sky. All of them were amazed by the bravery of this young child and were eager to help her on her journey.

Along the way, Rachel faced many challenges, but with the help of her new friends, she overcame them all. She had to cross treacherous rivers, climb steep mountains, and navigate through dark forests. Each obstacle she overcame made her stronger, braver, and more confident.

As the days turned into weeks, and the weeks into months, Rachel grew more and more determined to reach her destination. She knew that her journey was not yet over, but with every step she took, she came closer to achieving her goal.

Finally, after what seemed like an eternity, Rachel arrived at her destination. She stood in awe of the beautiful castle that stood before her, with its towering spires and glittering walls.

And as she stepped through the castle gates, she knew that her journey had been worth it.

For Rachel had not only discovered a magical world full of adventure and wonder, but she had also discovered something even more precious – herself. She had discovered that she was brave, resilient, and capable of achieving anything she set her mind to.

And so, with a heart full of joy and gratitude, Rachel realised that her journey was just the beginning of a new chapter in her life, one that was full of endless possibilities and magical adventures.

Obsessive-Compulsive Disorder (OCD)

Once upon a time, there was a young girl named Lana. She was a bright and curious child, always eager to explore the world around her. However, Lana struggled with a condition called obsessive-compulsive disorder (OCD), which made her feel anxious and trapped in repetitive thoughts and behaviours.

One day, a magical fairy appeared before Lana and whispered to her that there was a way to rid herself of her OCD. The fairy told her that she must embark on a journey to find the Golden Key, which would unlock a portal to a magical world where Lana's OCD could be vanquished forever.

Excited by the prospect of being free from her condition, Lana eagerly set out on her quest. She travelled through dark forests, across wide rivers, and over treacherous mountains. But every step of the way, her OCD tried to hold her back, with constant thoughts and compulsions.

At one point in her journey, Lana found herself trapped in a maze, where she was overwhelmed by thoughts of contamination and the need to wash her hands repeatedly. She began to feel hopeless, but then she remembered the fairy's words and took a deep breath. With each step, she repeated to herself, "I am strong, I am brave, and I can overcome this."

Finally, Lana arrived at the end of her journey, where she found the Golden Key. She inserted it into the lock, and the portal opened, revealing a beautiful, enchanted world. As she stepped through the portal, she felt a sense of relief and light wash over her. Her OCD was no longer there, and she was free to explore the magic of this new world.

Lana soon discovered that the magic of the world lay not only in its enchanting beauty but also in the support and guidance of the kind and caring people she met there. They helped her learn new ways to manage her thoughts and behaviours, and they showed her how to live a life full of joy and adventure, free from the constraints of her OCD.

From that day on, Lana knew that no matter what challenges she might face, she had the strength and courage to overcome them. She had learned to believe in herself and to trust in the magic of the world around her. And whenever she needed a reminder of that magic, she looked back on her journey and remembered the power of the Golden Key.

Losing Someone We Love

The trauma of losing something or someone significant during childhood can scar a person's psyche for a lifetime. The pain and grief of that experience can carve out a hollow space in their heart, leaving behind a sense of emotional emptiness that can be difficult to fill.

Even as they grow and mature, the memory of that loss can continue to shape their thoughts and feelings, shaping their perspective on the world around them.

The Magical Mirror of Healing

Once upon a time, in a far-off land, there lived a young girl named Jamie.

Jamie was a bright and bubbly child who loved to explore the world around her. She had a loving family with two parents who doted on her and an older brother who always looked out for her.

One day, tragedy struck when Jamie's mother passed away suddenly. Jamie was devastated. She couldn't understand why her mother had to leave her so soon. She felt lost and alone, and nothing seemed to make sense anymore.

But then, one night, Jamie had a dream. In her dream, she found herself in a magical forest, surrounded by trees that glowed with a soft, golden light. As she walked deeper into the forest, she saw a small cottage nestled among the trees.

As she approached the cottage, she saw that the door was ajar. She peeked inside and saw a kindly old woman sitting by the fire. The woman smiled warmly at Jamie and beckoned her inside.

"Hello, dear," the woman said. "I've been expecting you."

Jamie was surprised. "You have?" she asked.

The old woman nodded. "Yes, my child. I know why you're here. You're feeling lost and alone, aren't you?"

Jamie nodded, feeling a lump form in her throat.

The old woman stood up and walked over to Jamie. She took her hand and led her to a small room in the back of the cottage. Inside the room was a magical mirror, and as Jamie looked into it, she saw her mother smiling back at her.

"I know you miss your mother," the old woman said. "But she's never really left you. She's with you always, watching over you and guiding you. And whenever you feel sad or lonely, just look into this mirror, and she'll be here with you."

Jamie felt a warmth spread through her body, and she knew that the old woman was right. Her mother was still with her, even if she couldn't see her. She thanked the old woman and promised to always remember her words.

As Jamie walked back through the magical forest, she felt a sense of peace and comfort that she had never felt before. And from that day forward, whenever she missed her mother, she would look into the magical mirror and feel her mother's presence with her, guiding her through life's ups and downs.

Childhood Trauma

In a small town nestled deep in the woods, there lived a young boy named Raffin.

Raffin had a bright spirit and a contagious smile that lit up the room whenever he entered. However, he had experienced a great trauma in his childhood that had left him deeply scarred.

When Raffin was just seven years old, his parents died in a tragic accident, leaving him orphaned and alone. He was taken in by his aunt and uncle, who tried their best to provide for him. But Raffin couldn't shake off the feeling of abandonment and fear that haunted him every day. He stopped playing with his friends and stopped talking to his family. He felt like the whole world was against him.

One day, while wandering in the forest behind his house, Raffin stumbled upon a magical tree. The tree was unlike any other he had seen before, with shimmering leaves and a warm glow emanating from within. As he approached the tree, he felt a sense of comfort and safety wash over him.

As he reached out to touch the tree, a voice spoke to him. "What troubles you, child?" the voice asked.

Raffin was startled but found himself opening up to the tree. He told it everything - about his parents, his fears, and his feeling of loneliness. The tree listened patiently, and when Raffin finished, it spoke to him again.

"Child, you are not alone. You have a family who loves you, and I am here to protect you. Whenever you feel lost or afraid, come to me, and I will be your guide."

From that day on, Raffin visited the magical tree every day. He would sit under its branches, talk to it, and feel the warmth of its glow. Slowly but surely, he started to heal from his trauma. He started to play with his friends again, and he even began to smile and laugh more often.

As he grew older, Raffin never forgot the magical tree and the comfort it had brought him. Even as an adult, whenever he faced a difficult situation, he would close his eyes and think of the tree, and he would feel the same warmth and safety that he had felt as a child.

And so, the magical tree became a symbol of hope and healing for Raffin and for all those who had faced trauma in their lives. It reminded them that they were never alone and that there was always a way to heal and find happiness again.

Physical Pain

Frequent and Debilitating Migraines

Once upon a time, there was a young child who suffered from frequent and debilitating migraines. The child had tried every remedy and medication available, but nothing seemed to work. The pain would come on suddenly, and the child would be unable to do anything but lie in bed, clutching their head in agony.

One day, the child was out playing in the woods when they stumbled upon a beautiful fairy. The fairy saw the child's pain and asked what was wrong. The child explained their struggle with migraines, and the fairy knew just what to do.

The fairy took the child's hand and led them deep into the woods to a secret clearing. There, the fairy showed the child a magical plant that glowed with a soft, golden light.

The fairy explained that this plant was called the Migraine Flower, and it had the power to ease even the worst migraines.

The child was hesitant at first, but the fairy assured them that the plant was safe and that it had helped many others before. The child picked a few of the flowers and held them to their head. Almost instantly, the pain began to fade away. The child was amazed and grateful.

From that day on, the child kept a small bouquet of Migraine Flowers by their bedside, and whenever a migraine came on, they would hold the flowers to their head and feel the pain melt away. They never had to suffer from migraines again, and they knew that they had the fairy and the magical Migraine Flowers to thank for it.

Shyness

Let us embark on a journey of wonder and magic as you follow the incredible story of Sophie, a girl who was severely shy.

Once upon a time, there was a little girl named Sophie. She was a shy child who found it difficult to make friends and often felt left out. Her parents tried to help her by encouraging her to speak up and be more outgoing, but nothing seemed to work.

One day, as Sophie was walking through the forest near her home, she came across a tiny, glittering creature.

The creature introduced itself as a fairy and told Sophie that it had been watching her for some time. The fairy said that it had a gift for her, a magical potion that would help her overcome her shyness.

Sophie was sceptical but also intrigued. She took the potion and drank it, and suddenly she felt a rush of warmth and energy. The world around her seemed brighter, and she felt more confident and brave than ever before.

With her newfound courage, Sophie started to make friends and speak up more in class. She even joined the school play and performed in front of a big audience. Her parents were amazed at the transformation in their daughter, and Sophie felt like she could do anything.

But one day, as Sophie was playing in the forest, she saw the fairy again. The fairy looked sad and weak, and Sophie could tell that something was wrong. The fairy told her that the potion she had given her was made from a rare flower that only grew in the fairy kingdom. The flower was dying out because so many humans had been taking it, and the fairy was afraid that it would disappear forever.

Sophie felt terrible. She had never thought about where the potion had come from or how it had been made. She realised that she had been so focused on herself and her own needs that she had forgotten about the world around her.

Determined to make things right, Sophie went on a quest to find the fairy kingdom and help save the flower. She faced many challenges along the way, but with her newfound courage and determination, she was able to overcome them all.

In the end, Sophie found the fairy kingdom and was able to save the flower. The fairy thanked her and gave her a new potion, one that was made from the love and kindness of all the creatures in the forest.

Sophie drank the potion and felt a warm, happy feeling spreading through her body. She knew that she had learned an important lesson about the power of kindness and the importance of caring for the world around her.

From that day on, Sophie continued to be brave and outgoing, but she also made sure to be kind and thoughtful to others. She knew that true courage came from standing up for what was right and helping those in need, not just from being loud or confident.

And whenever she felt unsure or scared, she would remember the fairy's gift and the lessons she had learned, and she would feel a renewed sense of strength and purpose.

Bravery

A Dog Named Goldie.

Goldie was known as the protector of the village...

Once upon a time, in a far-off land, there was a beautiful dog named Goldie.

She had shiny, golden fur and big, soulful eyes that sparkled like diamonds. Goldie was the most loyal companion anyone could ever hope for, and she had a heart full of courage and love.

One sunny afternoon, Goldie was out for a walk with her owner when they heard a child's desperate cries for help. Without hesitation, Goldie took off running in the direction of the sound, her heart racing with determination.

When she arrived at the scene, Goldie saw a small child surrounded by a pack of ferocious wolves. The child was frozen with fear, and the wolves were closing in for the kill. But Goldie wasn't about to let that happen.

With a fierce bark, Goldie charged at the wolves, nipping at their heels and barking with all her might. The wolves were taken aback by Goldie bravery, and they hesitated for a moment. That was all the time Goldie needed to swoop in and grab the child by the scruff of the neck, whisking them away to safety.

Goldie had saved the child's life, and the villagers hailed her as a hero. From that day forward, she was known as the protector of the village, and she lived out the rest of her days basking in the love and adoration of the people she had saved.

And as for the child she had rescued, they never forgot the beautiful dog who had risked her life to save theirs. Goldie was a true hero, and her bravery and love would never be forgotten.

The Timid Mouse

The bravery of a little mouse named George...

In a magical forest deep within the Enchanted Kingdom, there was a little mouse named George.

George was a timid and shy mouse, but he had a heart full of bravery that he had yet to discover.

One day, while George was out foraging for food, he stumbled upon a squirrel named Robert. Robert was a big, burly squirrel with a mean streak.

He would intimidate George and pick on him every chance he got. Poor George was scared of Robert and didn't know what to do.

Feeling sad and alone, George went to see the wise old owl who lived in the tallest tree in the forest. The owl listened to George's troubles and gave him a magical potion to drink.

The potion was made from the tears of a unicorn and the wings of a fairy, and it had the power to give George the courage he needed to stand up to Robert.

With the potion in hand, George went back to face Robert. At first, Robert tried to bully George again, but then George drank the potion. Suddenly, he grew in size and strength, and his bravery soared to new heights. George challenged Robert to a fight, and the two faced off in a battle of wills.

Robert was surprised by George's newfound bravery and was no match for him. George emerged victorious and was no longer afraid of Robert. From that day on, George was known as the bravest mouse in the Enchanted Kingdom, and he lived happily ever after.

And so, dear friends, let this tale remind you that even the smallest and most timid among us can find the courage to face our fears and overcome them, thanks to the magic that lives within us all.

The Crystal Pendant

A special little girl named Leah who found the courage to fight back...

Once upon a time, in a mystical land filled with dragons and unicorns, there lived a young girl named Leah.

Leah had always been fascinated by the magic of the world around her, but she was too scared to try to use any magic of her own.

One day, while wandering through the enchanted forest, Leah came across a wise old sorceress named Morana.

Morana sensed the young girl's fear and knew that she had great potential as a powerful wizard. So, she took Leah under her wing and began to teach her the ways of magic.

At first, Leah struggled with even the simplest spells, but Morana saw something special in her and kept pushing her to practise. Eventually, Leah began to gain confidence and started to develop her own unique style of magic.

But then, an evil witch named Falen appeared in the land. Falen had an army of dark creatures at her command and she was determined to take over the kingdom and enslave its people.

Leah knew she had to act fast to stop her, but she was afraid she wasn't strong enough to face Falen and her minions.

Morana saw Leah's fear and gave her a magical crystal pendant that would boost her powers and give her the courage she needed to face Falen.

Leah put on the pendant and marched out to confront the witch. A fierce battle ensued, with bolts of lightning and blasts of fire raining down all around them.

Falen was a powerful adversary, but Leah fought with all her might and finally defeated her, banishing her and her army from the land forever.

From that day on, Leah was known as the greatest wizard in all the land, and she went on to have many more adventures and battles, always fighting for what was right and using her magic to protect the people she loved.

And she knew that she had Morana and the magic of her crystal pendant to thank for giving her the courage she needed to face any challenge that came her way.

The Power of Knowledge

Behold the immense might of knowledge! It possesses an unparalleled strength that can shatter the shackles of ignorance and enlighten the darkest of minds. The potency of knowledge transcends the physical realm and empowers individuals to achieve the impossible.

With knowledge as your weapon, you can conquer any challenge and overcome any obstacle that stands in your path. Harness the true potential of knowledge, and you shall unleash an unstoppable force that can change the course of history itself.

The Treasure of the Mind...

Once upon a time, there was a young adventurer named Azura who was always seeking the mysteries and treasures of the world. One day, while exploring a mystical forest, she stumbled upon an old, tattered map with the words "The Treasure of the Mind" written in shimmering silver ink.

Intrigued by the map's mystical aura, Azura followed its winding path, passing over mountains, through rivers and forests, and finally arriving at the entrance of a secret cave. The entrance was hidden behind a glistening waterfall, and Azura had to swim through the chilly water to enter.

As she walked deeper into the cave, Azura saw that the walls were covered in glowing runes and symbols. Suddenly, a beam of light shot out from one of the symbols and hit Azura, transporting her to a strange and wondrous place.

She found herself in a vast library filled with ancient books, scrolls, and mystical artefacts from all over the world. The shelves stretched up to the heavens, and Azura could see that there were endless levels of books, each containing vast knowledge and secrets.

In the centre of the library was a pedestal with a glowing, silver book resting on it. Azura approached the pedestal and opened the book, and was amazed to see that it contained all the knowledge she had ever sought.

The pages shimmered with a soft, mystical light, and as she read, she felt her mind expanding and becoming filled with endless wisdom.

But suddenly, she heard a deep, mystical voice from behind her. "Who dares to disturb the peace of this library?" Azura turned around and saw an old, wise-looking wizard standing behind her.

"I am Azura," she said, "and I have come in search of the Treasure of the Mind."

The wizard smiled and said, "You have found it, my dear Azura. The knowledge contained in this library is the greatest treasure of all."

Over the next few days, Azura read and studied the vast array of knowledge contained in the silver book. She learned about the secrets of the universe, the mysteries of magic, and the wonders of nature.

When she had finished, the wizard appeared once again and said, "Now that you have discovered the Treasure of the Mind, it is time for you to share it with the world."

And so, Azura left the library and travelled far and wide, spreading the knowledge she had gained to all those who would listen. She became a great mystic, sharing the secrets of the universe and helping others to discover the greatest treasure of all - the power of wisdom.

You can discover the secrets of the universe using knowledge as your weapon, and discover the magic within yourself...

The Magical Talisman

Once upon a time, there was a young girl named Celeste who lived in a small village on the edge of a vast forest. Celeste was always fascinated by stories of magic and the supernatural. She would spend hours reading books about witches, wizards, and enchanted creatures.

One day, while exploring the forest, Celeste stumbled upon a small, glittering object. As she picked it up, she felt a strange energy coursing through her body. She realised that the object was a magical talisman that had been hidden deep within the forest.

From that moment on, Celeste's life was forever changed. She began to notice that she had a special connection to the natural world around her. She could sense the presence of animals and plants, and she seemed to be able to communicate with them in some way.

As time passed, Celeste learned to harness her newfound powers. She discovered that she had the ability to cast spells and create powerful charms. She used her magic to help others, healing sick animals and tending to the needs of the plants and trees in the forest.

One day, an evil sorcerer came to the village, threatening to destroy everything in his path. The villagers were afraid and didn't know what to do. But Celeste knew that she had to act fast. She called upon her magical powers, and with a single spell, she was able to defeat the sorcerer and save the village.

From that day forward, Celeste was hailed as a hero. She had discovered the magic within herself, and she had used it to protect those she loved. She continued to explore the forest, discovering new and exciting things every day.

And although she knew that there would always be challenges to face, she was never afraid, knowing that the magic within her would always guide her on the right path.

The Tree of Knowledge

In a small village nestled deep in the heart of a lush green forest, there was a little boy named Tommy. Tommy was a curious child, always asking questions and eager to learn about the world around him.

One day, as Tommy was exploring the forest, he stumbled upon a magical tree. The tree was unlike any other he had ever seen, with branches that reached up towards the sky and roots that delved deep into the earth.

As he gazed up at the tree, Tommy felt a strange sensation wash over him. It was as if the tree was speaking to him, whispering secrets and knowledge that he had never known before.

With each passing moment, Tommy felt his mind expanding, growing and changing as he absorbed the knowledge that the tree was sharing with him. He learned about the mysteries of the universe, the wonders of science, and the secrets of the human heart.

And as he learned, Tommy began to understand who he truly was, and what he was capable of. He discovered his passions, his strengths, and his weaknesses, and he learned how to harness them to achieve his dreams.

In time, Tommy grew up to become a wise and knowledgeable adult, always seeking out new knowledge and eager to share what he had learned with others.

He never forgot the lessons he had learned from the magical tree, and he always remembered to approach the world with the curiosity and wonder of a child.

And so, my friend, the story of Tommy teaches us that the mind of a child is a powerful thing, full of potential and endless possibility. By embracing our inner child and seeking out knowledge with an open heart and mind, we too can discover our true selves and unlock our full potential.

The journey is more important than the destination...

The Journey of Learning

In a realm beyond time and space, where the stars danced to a cosmic melody, there was a child named Celeste who was about to embark on an enchanting journey of learning.

Celeste lived in a cottage surrounded by a garden of twinkling flowers, where the trees whispered secrets to each other, and the creatures of the night sang sweet melodies. One evening, as she was watching the stars, a glowing spirit appeared before her.

"Greetings, Celeste," the spirit said. "I am the Guardian of Knowledge, and I have come to take you on a mystical journey."

Celeste's eyes widened with wonder as the Guardian took her by the hand and led her into the garden. The flowers shimmered and swayed as they walked, and the fireflies lit the way.

"Close your eyes and make a wish," the Guardian whispered, and Celeste closed her eyes tightly, imagining all the things she wanted to learn and discover.

Suddenly, she felt a rush of wind, and when she opened her eyes, she found herself in a magical hall, filled with books from every realm and every era. The Guardian smiled and said, "This is the Hall of Enchantment, where you can learn anything your heart desires."

Excitedly, Celeste ran to a shelf and pulled out a book on the language of the stars. As she turned the pages, the constellations shone brighter and brighter, and she found herself in a realm of pure light, surrounded by celestial beings. She learned all about the secrets of the universe and the patterns of the stars.

Next, she chose a book on ancient magic, and suddenly she was transported to a realm of pure magic, where she learned how to harness the elements and cast spells. She marvelled at the power and beauty of enchantment.

As the night went on, Celeste explored more books on mythology, art, philosophy, and other mystical subjects, each time transported to a new world of learning and wonder. The Guardian watched over her, guiding her and answering her questions.

Finally, as the night began to fade, the Guardian said, "It's time to go home, Celeste. But remember, this journey of learning is just the beginning. The universe is full of magic and wonder to discover, and you can learn something new every day."

Celeste hugged the Guardian tightly and thanked her for the enchanting journey. As she walked back to her cottage, she felt a sense of awe and curiosity in her heart, eager to explore the universe and learn more.

From that night on, Celeste embraced every opportunity to learn, whether it was through books, experiences, or interactions with other beings. And she knew that as long as she kept an open mind and a thirst for knowledge, her journey of enchantment would continue to be a wondrous and inspiring one.

The Meaning of Life.

In a world much like our own, there was a young wizard named Arin. Arin was a curious and adventurous wizard who spent most of his time exploring the magical forests and mountains of his land.

One day, as Arin was walking through the woods, he stumbled upon a wise old sage sitting by a tree. The sage was deep in thought, and Arin couldn't help but wonder what was troubling him.

"Excuse me, sir," Arin said, "Is everything alright?"

The sage looked up and smiled at Arin. "Yes, my child," he said. "I was just pondering the meaning of life."

"The meaning of life?" Arin asked, intrigued.

"Yes," the sage replied. "I have been searching for the answer for many years, but I have yet to find it. Perhaps you can help me?"

Arin was taken aback. He was just a young wizard, how could he possibly know the answer to such a profound question?

But the sage looked at him with kind eyes and said, "You may be surprised at what you can learn if you keep an open mind and listen with your heart."

Arin sat down beside the sage, and together they began to contemplate the meaning of life. They talked for hours, exploring various ideas and philosophies, but still, they couldn't come to a satisfactory answer.

As the sun began to set, Arin suddenly had an idea. "What if," he said, "the meaning of life is not something we can find, but something we must create?"

The sage looked at him, intrigued. "What do you mean?"

Arin explained that life is like a blank canvas, and we are the artists who must paint our own pictures. The meaning of life, then, is to create a life that is meaningful and fulfilling to us.

The sage thought about this for a moment and then nodded. "I think you may be onto something, my young friend. Life is what we make of it, and it is up to us to create something beautiful."

From that day on, Arin and the sage became good friends, and they continued to explore the meaning of life together. And although they never found a definitive answer, they realised that the journey was more important than the destination.

Arin went on to become one of the greatest wizards of his time, known not only for his magical abilities but also for his wisdom and compassion. And he knew that the true meaning of life was to live it with purpose and love, to create something beautiful that would last long after he was gone.

Happiness: The Joy of Being Alive

In a world of endless possibilities, there lived a child whose heart burned with a fierce desire for happiness. This child was unlike any other, for they possessed a rare gift: the ability to see the magic and wonder in the world around them.

Driven by an insatiable thirst for happiness, the child set out on a quest to discover the secrets of true joy. With each step, the child felt the weight of the world lift from their shoulders, as if the very act of seeking had set them free.

Through enchanted forests and across treacherous oceans, the child journeyed, facing challenges and overcoming obstacles with a sense of purpose and determination. Along the way, the child met many wise sages and mystical creatures who offered guidance and insight into the nature of happiness.

As the child travelled deeper into the unknown, the magic of the world began to reveal itself, and the child's heart swelled with wonder and awe. Each new discovery brought the child closer to the truth, until finally, the child arrived at the threshold of the fabled land of happiness.

With a trembling heart, the child crossed the threshold and beheld a world of wonder and delight. Yet, as the child explored this magical land, they realised that the true source of happiness lay not in the world around them, but within themselves.

Filled with this realisation, the child returned home, forever changed by the magic of their journey. And from that day forward, the child lived each moment with a sense of wonder and gratitude, knowing that the key to true happiness lay not in what they possessed, but in the simple joy of being alive.

The Storyteller's Tale

The mystery that hides within every one of us has the power to inspire and transform our lives...

In a distant realm, beyond the horizon of what most mortals had ever seen, there existed a magical kingdom filled with wonders and mysteries. And in this kingdom, there lived a young prince named Liam.

Liam was not like the other princes in the kingdom. He had a secret that he kept hidden from everyone else. He had a magical story that lived inside him, one that contained hidden meanings and symbols that only he could decipher.

As Liam grew older, his story began to unfold. He discovered that he had a special gift for storytelling, and his words had the power to transport people to different worlds and realms.

His stories were filled with magic and wonder, and they held within them the secrets of his soul.

One day, Liam decided to share his stories with the people of his kingdom. He stood in the town square and began to weave his tale, and as he spoke, the people listened in awe. They were enchanted by his words, and they could feel the power of his story resonating within them.

As he finished his tale, Liam realised that his story was not just his own. It was a story that belonged to everyone in the kingdom, a tale of triumphs and challenges, of joy and sorrow, of love and loss. And as he looked out at the faces of the people in the town square, he knew that his story had the power to inspire and transform their lives.

And so, Liam continued to share his story with the people of his kingdom, and as he did, he watched as they became more connected to each other and to the magic that lived within them. He knew that his story was not just a tale, but a gift, one that he would continue to share with the world for all time.

The Magical Forest

A magical forest where the dreams of children come alive...

Every night, as the children drifted off to sleep, their dreams would take them to this enchanted place where they could explore, play, and let their imaginations run wild.

In the centre of the forest, there was a giant tree that was said to hold the key to unlocking the greatest dreams. This tree was guarded by a group of friendly fairies who would guide the children through the forest and help them discover their true passions.

One night, a young boy named George had a dream about the magical forest. He dreamed of running through the fields of wildflowers, climbing the trees, and swimming in the crystal-clear lake. He felt a sense of freedom and joy he had never experienced before.

As George explored the forest, he came across the giant tree. The fairies appeared and led him to the tree's entrance, where he saw a glowing keyhole. With a magical key that the fairies gave him, George unlocked the tree and stepped inside.

Inside the tree, George discovered a room filled with all of his wildest dreams. There were shelves lined with books, walls covered in paintings, and musical instruments scattered throughout the room. George felt overwhelmed with excitement and wonder as he explored this magical place.

As he played the instruments, read the books, and admired the paintings, George realised that his true passion was to become a musician. He had always loved music but never had the confidence to pursue it.

With the encouragement of the fairies, George decided to follow his dream and become a musician. He practised every day and eventually became a famous musician, inspiring others to follow their dreams.

And so, the children of the world continued to visit the magical forest in their dreams, unlocking their true passions and achieving their wildest dreams, all thanks to the power of imagination and the magic of the enchanted forest.

Becoming Calm

This is the story of Leo, a little boy who finally learned to control his anger...

In a realm beyond the veil of mortal sight, where the shimmering stars met the edge of the cosmos, there lived a child named Leo.

Leo was always angry, no matter what happened. He would yell and scream, and throw things when he was upset. His parents didn't know what to do, and neither did his teachers or friends.

One day, while Leo was on a walk in the woods, he stumbled upon a magical pond. The water was crystal clear, and there were lily pads floating on the surface. Leo sat down by the pond and looked at his reflection. He saw a scowl on his face and tears in his eyes.

As he sat there, he noticed something strange happening. The water in the pond began to swirl and a small creature emerged. It was a fairy, and she had come to help Leo with his anger.

The fairy told Leo that she could show him a way to find inner peace, but he would have to follow her instructions carefully. Leo was willing to try anything, so he agreed to the fairy's plan.

The fairy took Leo by the hand and led him to a nearby tree. She told him to sit down and close his eyes. Then, she instructed him to take deep breaths and imagine himself in a peaceful place.

Leo did as he was told, and soon he found himself in a beautiful garden. The flowers were in bloom, and the sun was shining. He felt happy and calm and his anger began to dissipate.

The fairy explained to Leo that this garden was his own mind, and that he could visit it whenever he felt angry or upset. All he had to do was close his eyes and take deep breaths.

From that day on, Leo visited his garden whenever he felt angry. He learned to take deep breaths and calm himself down. He found that he was able to handle his emotions better, and that his anger no longer controlled him.

Leo's parents noticed a change in him, and they were amazed. They asked him what had happened, and he told them about the magical pond and the fairy who had helped him find inner peace.

From then on, Leo lived a much happier life, and he knew that he would always have his peaceful garden to visit whenever he needed it.

Immerse yourself in magical tales of self-discovery that go beyond mere imagination. Each story is a carefully crafted work of fiction interwoven with threads of inspiration, taking you on a journey of wonder and possibility.

The stories I have shared are works of fiction that aim to take readers on a journey to imaginary worlds full of wonder and magic. Although the events portrayed are not based on real-life occurrences, they touch on important themes, such as self-discovery and the strength of the human mind.

Even though the stories contain fantastical elements, they still hold valuable lessons that can be applied in real life. Through the tales, readers are encouraged to reflect on the power of their thoughts and emotions and how they can impact their well-being.

Essentially, whilst these stories may not be factual, they can inspire us to explore our own minds and unleash our own inner transformative ability.

The Thirty-Day Challenge for Children

Have you ever heard of a magical challenge that can make your wishes come true? It's called the Thirty-Day Challenge!

How it Works

First, you get to write down on a special card or piece of paper exactly what you really, really want. It can be anything you wish for, like a new toy, a pet, or even a trip to Disneyland! And guess what? You get to keep that card with you all the time, even when you go to bed at night!

Then, for the next 30 days, you get to repeat your wish out loud 30 times a day! But wait; that's not all! You have to do more than just say it; you have to really believe in it! Imagine what it would be like if your wish came true, feel it in your heart, and see it in your mind's eye.

And here's the most exciting part! When you keep doing this every day for 30 days, without missing even one day, something magical happens! Our thoughts are super powerful, and they can create our reality! That means if you truly believe in your wish, you can make it come true!

So, are you ready for the Thirty-Day Challenge? Remember, focus on one wish at a time, and believe in it with all your heart! Let's make your dreams come true!

Start your challenge now…

1. Write down on a special card or piece of paper exactly what you really want.
2. Then, for the next 30 days, you get to repeat your wish out loud 30 times a day!
3. Really believe in it! Imagine what it would be like if your wish came true.
4. Focus on one wish at a time.

Our Thoughts

Our thoughts hold an incredible power to shape the world around us. From the smallest seed of an idea can grow the most magnificent of realities. We hold within us the ability to bring our deepest desires to fruition through the unwavering belief in our thoughts. So, let us dream without limits and let our thoughts soar to new heights. With each thought, we pave the way for the life we truly deserve. Let us embrace this power within us and create a world beyond our wildest imaginations.

Mystical 30-Day Adventure

The Magical Thirty-Day Challenge using the power of your mind...

Once upon a time, in a land of magic and mystery, there was a fabled challenge known as the Mystical 30-Day Adventure. It was whispered that this adventure held the key to unlocking any wish.

One day, a young adventurer named Abby stumbled upon a mysterious book that contained the instructions for the Mystical

30-Day Adventure. With a heart full of wonder and excitement, Abby knew she had to take on this challenge and see if it was truly magical.

She took out a special piece of paper and wrote down her deepest desire on it. It was a dream she had held close to her heart for a long time - to be able to talk to fairies and experience their enchanted world. With the paper in hand, Abby began the adventure.

For the next 30 days, Abby repeated her wish out loud 30 times a day. But it wasn't enough to just say it - she had to truly believe it with all her heart. And so she did. She closed her eyes and imagined herself surrounded by fairies, hearing their laughter and feeling the sparkle of magic all around her.

As the days went by, something began to shift within Abby. She started to notice that the world around her was becoming more and more enchanted. Flowers bloomed in the most unexpected places, the leaves on the trees seemed to shimmer with a new light, and tiny fairy houses appeared in the nooks and crannies of the forest.

And then, in a burst of mystical energy, Abby suddenly found herself transported into the world of the fairies! She danced with them, played games with them, and listened to their songs. Her wish had come true, thanks to the power of the Mystical 30-Day Adventure!

From that day on, Abby knew that anything was possible if she just believed in it with all her heart. And she continued to use the magic of the Mystical 30-Day Adventure to make her dreams a reality, one adventure at a time.

Words of wisdom

Remember you are special.

I want to remind you that even if you're young and going through difficult times, you possess a remarkable strength that will carry you through the darkest of moments. You are not only strong and amazing, but you are an angel walking the earth, here for a purpose that only you can fulfil.

Remember that your past experiences are valuable lessons that have helped shape you into the person you are today. Embrace this moment as a precious gift, one that you can use to continue growing and developing the inner strength that lies within you.

As you journey through life, know that there will be ups and downs, twists and turns, but trust that you are being guided to exactly where you are meant to be. Embrace the journey, and let it lead you to the purpose that is waiting for you.

And most importantly, know that no matter what life throws your way, you have the ability and the courage to overcome anything.

Hold on to that inner strength and belief in yourself, for it will always be there to guide you through the toughest of times.

And So The Journey Begins...

I hope you enjoyed the magical stories of make believe. As you may have noticed, there is a deeper meaning to every story that goes beyond the surface level plot. These meanings can be interpreted differently by different readers, and each person's interpretation is unique to their own experiences, perspectives, and emotions.

By immersing yourself in the world of make-believe, you open yourself up to a world of possibility and imagination. You allow yourself to explore new ideas and concepts in a safe and enjoyable way, which can inspire you to think differently and approach challenges with a fresh perspective.

Whether it's a story about a brave hero overcoming impossible odds or a fable about the consequences of greed and selfishness, each tale has something to offer. It's up to you to reflect on the meaning behind the story and how it relates to your own life.

So, I encourage you to continue reading and exploring the wonderful world of literature. You never know what insights and inspirations you may uncover along the way!

The next step is to speak to one of our dedicated practitioners who have been trained by me in Inherited Therapy and The Loveday Method.

There you have it; the help you desperately need is here, to visit the people you have lost.

So let the journey begin.

For more information visit these sites.
https://www.inheritedtherapy.com
https://www.liverpoolhypnosis.co.uk

Or contact me on:
geof@inheritedtherapy.com

❖

Look out for my next book, the Fifth in the series of Seven, Coming Out in March 2024.

How To Reverse Disease In The Body?

The Loveday Method
Part 5

Do your thoughts have the power to heal you? Or can your thoughts fuel disease?

Just suppose you could reverse disease in the body.

This is an interesting concept.

So get my next book to find the answers.

Milton Keynes UK
Ingram Content Group UK Ltd.
UKHW051941160124
436136UK00004B/81